Handwriting Practice:
From the Bible!

Book 1

Brookdale House
A Curriculum Publishing Company

BOOKS PUBLISHED BY BROOKDALE HOUSE:

The Writing Through Ancient History books
Writing Through Ancient History Level 1 Cursive Models
Writing Through Ancient History Level 1 Manuscript Models
Writing Through Ancient History Level 2 Cursive Models
Writing Through Ancient History Level 2 Manuscript Models

The Writing Through Medieval History books
Writing Through Medieval History Level 1 Cursive Models
Writing Through Medieval History Level 1 Manuscript Models
Writing Through Medieval History Level 2 Cursive Models
Writing Through Medieval History Level 2 Manuscript Models

The Writing Through Early Modern History Books
Writing Through Early Modern History Level 1 Cursive Models
Writing Through Early Modern History Level 1 Manuscript Models
Writing Through Early Modern History Level 2 Cursive Models
Writing Through Early Modern History Level 2 Manuscript Models

The Writing Through Modern History Books
Writing Through Modern History Level 1 Cursive Models
Writing Through Modern History Level 1 Manuscript Models
Writing Through Modern History Level 2 Cursive Models
Writing Through Modern History Level 2 Manuscript Models

The Fun Spanish Level 1
(Introductory Spanish workbook for elementary students)

Sheldon's Primary Language Lessons
(Introductory grammar workbook for elementary students)

The Westminster Shorter Catechism Copybook
(Available in the following: traditional, modern, italic, and vertical, both print and cursive)

Bible Memorization Made Easy
(Memorize Galatians, Memorize Philippians, Memorize Psalms for Praying, and Memorize the Sermon on the Mount.)

ISBN-13: 978-1-64281-021-9

© Copyright 2014 by Brookdale House: A Curriculum Publishing Company.

Brookdale House grants permission to photocopy pages for use within a single family. All other rights reserved. No part of this publication may be reproduced by any means without the prior written permission of the copyright owner. For permission to make copies, written or otherwise, except for the use within one immediate family, please contact the author at www.brookdalehouse.com or Kimberly@brookdalehouse.com .

BACKGROUND

The Bible Handwriting Practice series provides children with handwriting exercises that contain Christian content. In Book 1 Children learn to form their letters and practice writing words such as:

Adam	God	Mary	Sheep	Yoke
Book	Holy	Noah	Truth	Zion
Child	Israel	Obey	Unto	
David	Jesus	Pray	Voice	
Eden	King	Quiet	Wait	
Faith	Lamb	Risen	Xerxes	

In addition to the penmanship practice, Scripture relevant to the handwriting models are included with each letter, providing instructors with the opportunity to teach proper penmanship and Bible literacy.

INSTRUCTIONS

This handwriting workbook is divided into four sections. Spend as much time as your student needs in any area. Older students may spend one or two days on a letter or page. Younger students may spend as much as a week.

Quality over quantity!

Writing Letters

In this section, students become familiar with forming the letters of the alphabet.

Writing Words

As students write words form the Bible, they focus primarily on one letter of the alphabet, reinforcing proper letter formation.

Additional time may be spent on the Scripture passage located at the top of each page. By simply reading and discussing the Bible verses with your students, you will teach them to recognize Biblical references, or allusions, when they encounter them in their reading material.

Reviewing Letters

In this section, students develop writing fluency by copying all of the letters of the alphabet. These smaller letters contain arrows, reminding students how to form each letter properly.

Writing Numbers

In this section, students learn to write the numbers 0 to 9.

Writing Scripture

In this short section, students copy short passages of Scripture taken from their previous letter writing lessons. Younger students may spend one or more days tracing the gray Scripture passage. When they are ready, they spend one or more days copying the second version of the passage.

This section takes approximately 4 weeks to complete; it is included to aid children in transitioning from *Handwriting Practice: From the Bible! Book 1* to *Handwriting Practice: From the Bible! Book 2*.

TABLE OF CONTENTS:

Scripture ix

Writing Letters 1

    Forming the Letters 2

    Forming the Letters 9

Writing Words 17

    The Letter A 18

    The Letter B 19

    The Letter C 20

    The Letter D 21

    The Letter E 22

    The Letter F 23

    The Letter G 24

    The Letter H 25

    The Letter I 26

    The Letter J 27

    The Letter K 28

    The Letter L 29

    The Letter M 30

    The Letter N 31

    The Letter O 32

    The Letter P 33

    The Letter Q 34

    The Letter R 35

    The Letter S 36

The Letter T	37
The Letter U	38
The Letter V	39
The Letter W	40
The Letter X	41
The Letter Y	42
The Letter Z	43
Reviewing	**45**
Reviewing the Letters	46
Reviewing the Letters	47
Reviewing the Letters	48
Reviewing the Letters	49
Writing Numbers	**51**
Writing Scripture	**61**
Day 1: Genesis 1:1 Word Practice	62
Day 2: Genesis 1:1 Word Practice	63
Day 3: Genesis 1:1 Word Practice	64
Day 4: Genesis 1:1	65
Day 1: Isaiah 9:6 Word Practice	66
Day 2: Isaiah 9:6 Word Practice	67
Day 3: Isaiah 9:6 Word Practice	68
Day 4: Isaiah 9:6	69
Day 1: John 10:27 Word Practice	70
Day 2: John 10:27 Word Practice	71
Day 3: John 10:27 Word Practice	72
Day 4: John 10:27	73

Day 1: Isaiah 6:3 Word Practice 74
Day 2: Isaiah 6:3 Word Practice 75
Day 3: Isaiah 6:3 Word Practice 76
Day 4: Isaiah 6:3 77

SCRIPTURE

The following Bible verses are included with the letter writing practice. These verses have been added to give students exposure to common Biblical allusions and increase their Bible literacy.

Students are not expected to be able to read the Scripture by themselves. Instructors will read the Bible verse to the students.

A   And **Adam** gave names to all cattle, and to the fowl of the air, and to every beast of the field. Genesis 2:20

B   And the Lord said unto Moses, write this for a memorial in a **book**. Exodus 17:14

C   For unto us a **child** is born, unto us a son is given. Isaiah 9:6

D   **David** said moreover, The Lord that delivered me out of the paw of the lion, and out of the paw of the bear, he will deliver me out of the hand of this Philistine. 1 Samuel 17:37

E   And the Lord God took the man, and put him into the Garden of **Eden** to dress it and to keep it. Genesis 2:15

F   Now **faith** is the substance of things hoped for, the evidence of things not seen. Hebrews 11:1

G   In the beginning **God** created the heaven and the earth. Genesis 1:1

H   And one cried unto another, and said, "**Holy**, **holy**, **holy** is the LORD of hosts. The whole earth is full of his glory." Isaiah 6:3

I   And he said, "Thy name shall be called no more Jacob, but **Israel**: for as a prince hast thou power with God and with men, and hast prevailed." Genesis 32:28

J   And she shall bring forth a son, and thou shalt call his name **Jesus**: for he shall save his people from their sins. Matthew 1:21

K   The **king** answered unto Daniel, and said, "Of a truth it is, that your God is a God of gods, and a Lord of kings, and a revealer of secrets, seeing that thou couldest reveal this secret." Daniel 2:47

L The next day John seeth Jesus coming unto him, and saith, "Behold the **Lamb** of God, who taketh away the sin of the world." John 1:29

M And they came with haste, and found **Mary**, and Joseph, and the babe lying in a manger. Luke 2:16

N And God blessed **Noah** and his sons, and said unto them, "Be fruitful, and multiply, and replenish the earth." Genesis 9:1

O Then Peter and the other apostles answered and said, "We ought to **obey** God rather than men." Acts 5:29

P Rejoice evermore. **Pray** without ceasing. In everything give thanks, for this is the will of God in Christ Jesus concerning you.
1 Thessalonians 5:16-18

Q The words of wise men are heard in **quiet** more than the cry of him that ruleth among fools. Ecclesiastes 9:17

R He is not here: for he is **risen**, as he said. Come; see the place where the Lord lay. Matthew 28:6

S My **sheep** hear my voice, and I know them, and they follow me. John 10:27

T Jesus saith unto him, "I am the way, the **truth**, and the life: no man cometh unto the Father, but by me." John 14:6

U **Unto** thee, O my strength, will I sing: for God is my defense, and the God of my mercy. Psalm 59:17

V When Moses saw it, he wondered at the sight: and as he drew near to behold it, the **voice** of the Lord came unto him, Acts 7:31

W But they that **wait** upon the LORD shall renew their strength; they shall mount up with wings as eagles; they shall run, and not be weary; and they shall walk, and not faint. Isaiah 40:31

X I also and my maidens will fast likewise; and so will I go in unto the king (King **Xerxes**), which is not according to the law: and if I perish, I perish. Esther 4:16

Y   Take My **yoke** upon you and learn of Me, for I am meek and lowly in heart, and ye shall find rest unto your souls. For My **yoke** is easy, and My burden is light. Matthew 11:28-30

Z   Praise the Lord, O Jerusalem! Praise thy God, O **Zion**! Psalm 147:12

WRITING LETTERS

FORMING THE LETTERS

Trace the letters as neatly as you can.

Copy the letters on the lines provided.

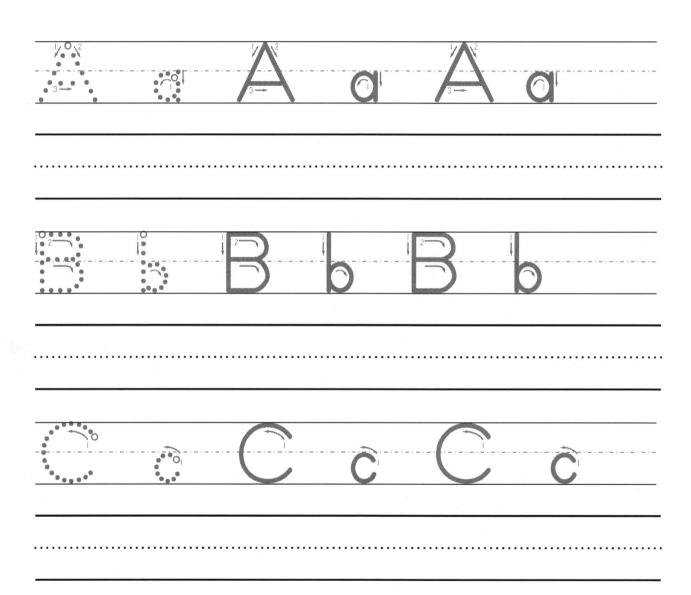

2

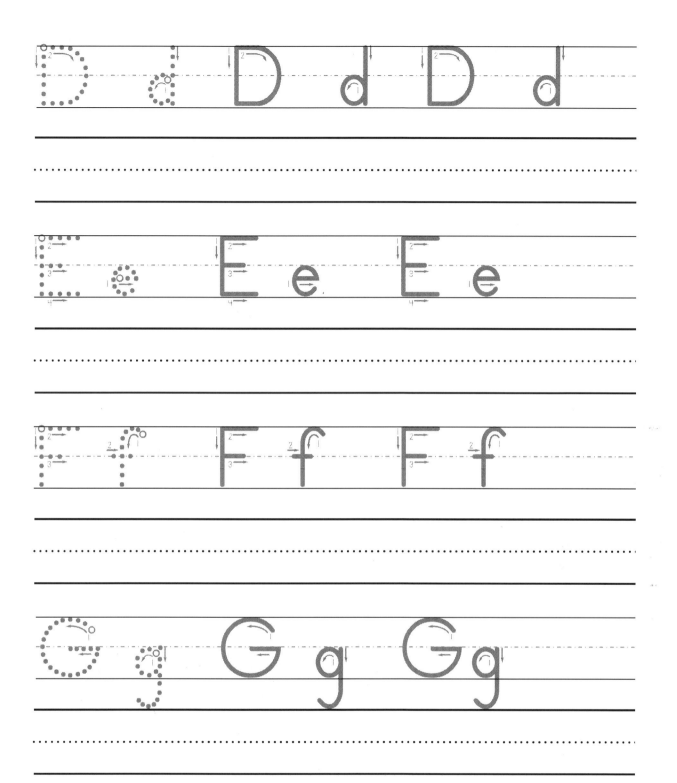

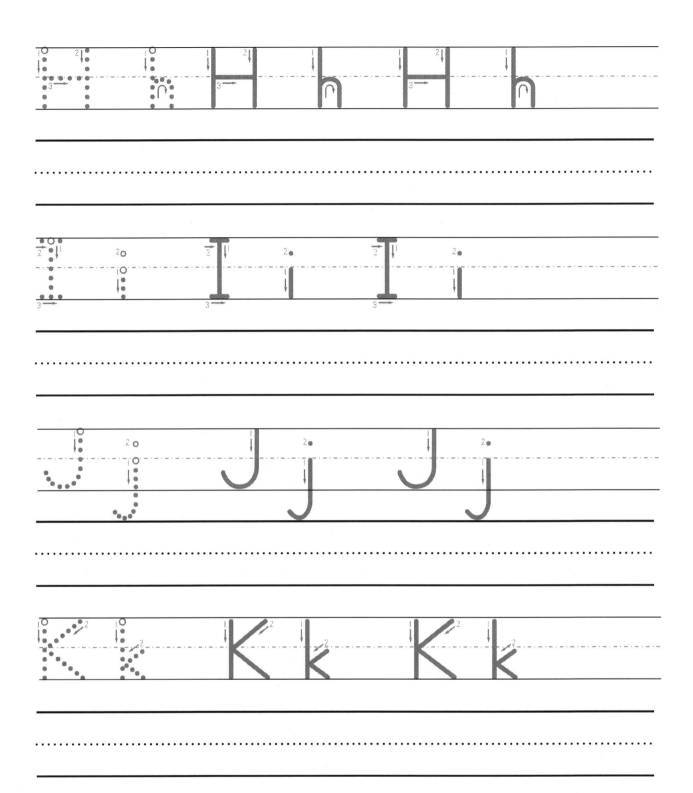

Ll Ll Ll Ll

Mm Mm Mm Mm

Nn Nn Nn Nn

Oo Oo Oo Oo

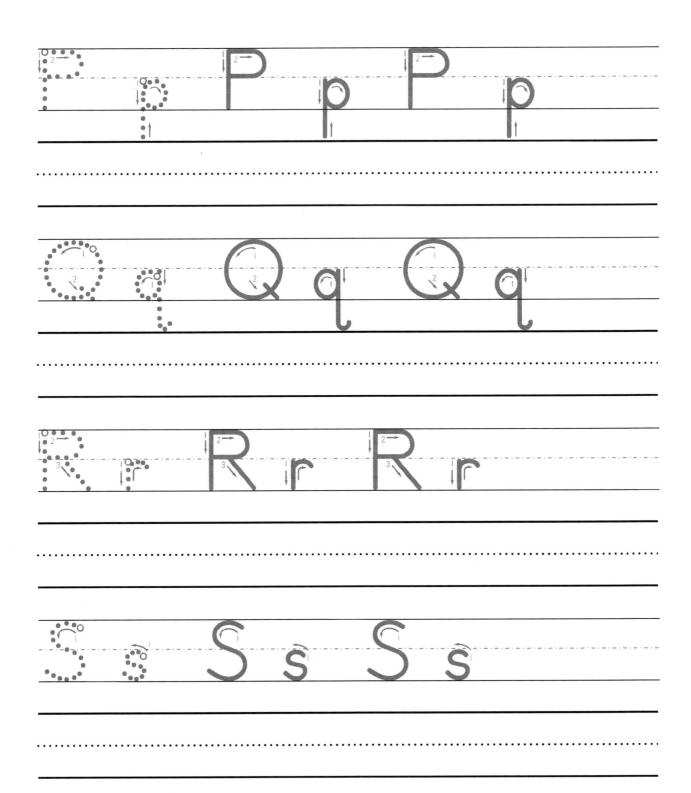

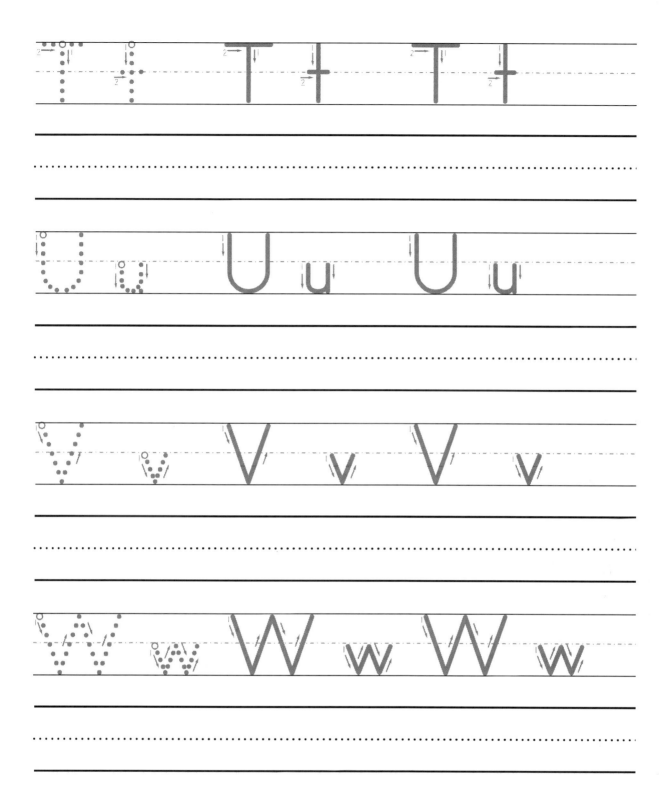

FORMING THE LETTERS

For additional practice, if needed, trace any or all of the letters as neatly as you can.

Copy them on the lines provided.

A a A a A a

B b B b B b

C c C c C c

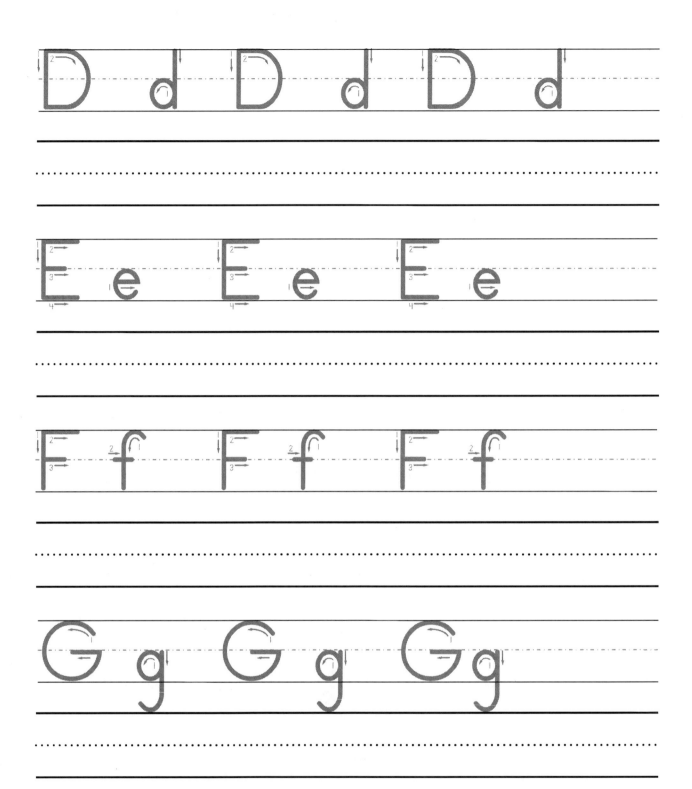

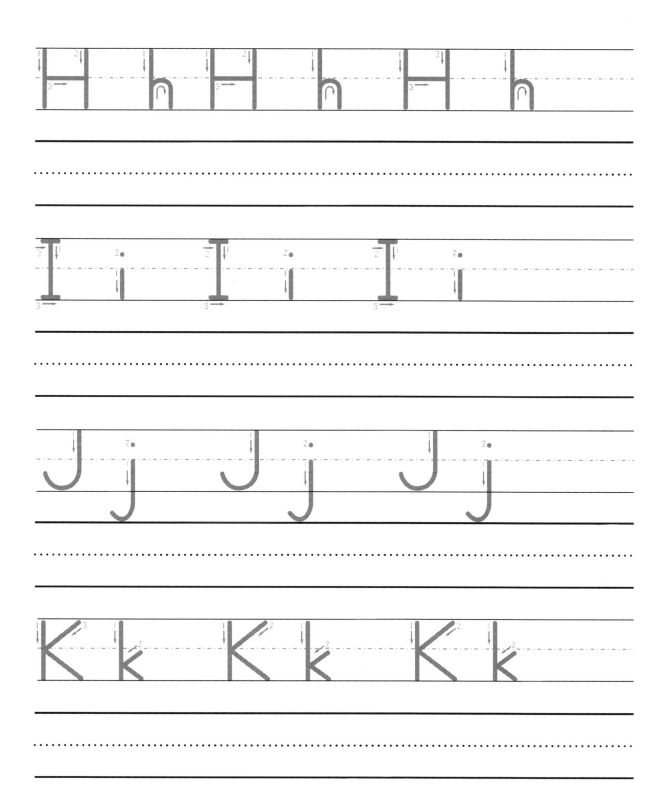

L l L l L l

M m M m M m

N n N n N n

O o O o O o

P p P p P p

Q q Q q Q q

R r R r R r

S s S s S s

Tt Tt Tt

Uu Uu Uu

Vv Vv Vv

Ww Ww Ww

X x X x X x

Y y Y y Y y

Z z Z z Z z

WRITING WORDS

THE LETTER A

And **Adam** gave names to all cattle, and to the fowl of the air, and to every beast of the field. Genesis 2:20

1) Neatly trace the letters.
2) On the lines provided, copy the letters in your neatest handwriting.

Aa Aa Aa Aa Aa

Aa Aa Aa Aa Aa

Adam Adam Adam

Adam Adam Adam

THE LETTER B

And the Lord said unto Moses, write this for a memorial in a **book**. Exodus 17:14

1) Neatly trace the letters.
2) On the lines provided, copy the letters in your neatest handwriting.

Bb Bb Bb Bb

Bb Bb Bb Bb

Book Book Book

Book Book Book

The Letter C

For unto us a **child** is born, unto us a son is given.
Isaiah 9:6

1) Neatly trace the letters.
2) On the lines provided, copy the letters in your neatest handwriting.

C c C c C c C c

C c C c C c C c

Child Child Child

Child Child Child

20

THE LETTER D

David said moreover, The Lord that delivered me out of the paw of the lion, and out of the paw of the bear, he will deliver me out of the hand of this Philistine. I Samuel 17:37

1) Neatly trace the letters.
2) On the lines provided, copy the letters in your neatest handwriting.

D d   D d   D d   D d

D d   D d   D d   D d

David David David

David David David

THE LETTER E

And the Lord God took the man, and put him into the Garden of **Eden** to dress it and to keep it. Genesis 2:15

1) Neatly trace the letters.
2) On the lines provided, copy the letters in your neatest handwriting.

Ee Ee Ee Ee Ee

Ee Ee Ee Ee

Eden Eden Eden

Eden Eden Eden

THE LETTER F

Now **faith** is the substance of things hoped for, the evidence of things not seen. Hebrews 11:1

1) Neatly trace the letters.
2) On the lines provided, copy the letters in your neatest handwriting.

THE LETTER G

In the beginning **God** created the heaven and the earth. Genesis 1:1

1) Neatly trace the letters.
2) On the lines provided, copy the letters in your neatest handwriting.

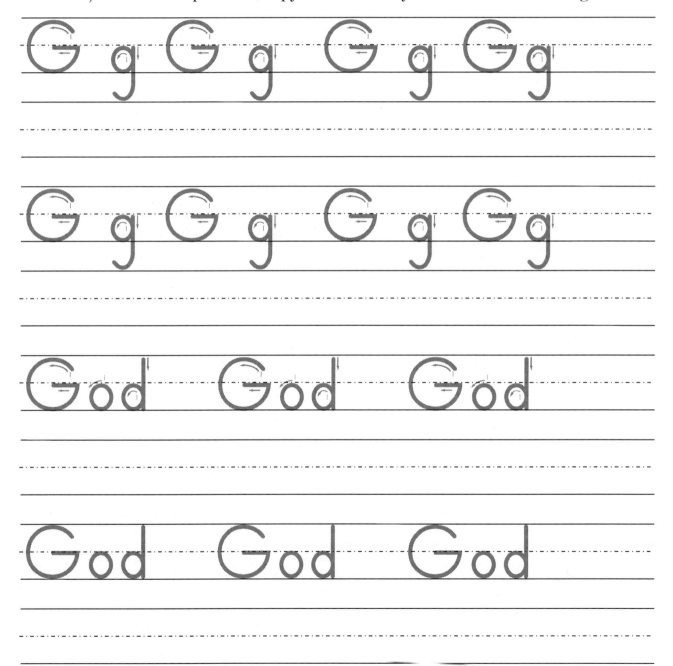

THE LETTER H

And one cried unto another, and said, "Holy, holy, holy is the LORD of hosts. The whole earth is full of his glory." Isaiah 6:3

1) Neatly trace the letters.
2) On the lines provided, copy the letters in your neatest handwriting.

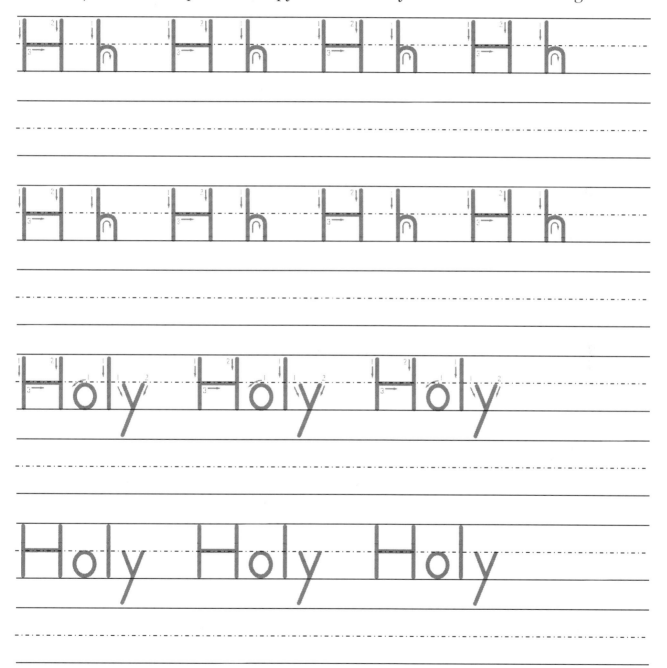

THE LETTER I

And he said, "Thy name shall be called no more Jacob, but Israel: for as a prince hast thou power with God and with men, and has prevailed." Genesis 32:28

1) Neatly trace the letters.
2) On the lines provided, copy the letters in your neatest handwriting.

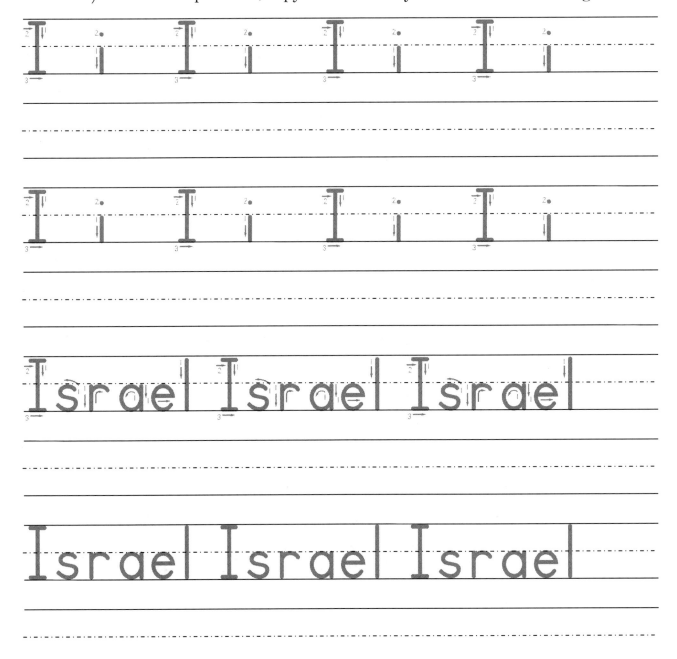

THE LETTER J

And she shall bring forth a son, and thou shall call his name **Jesus**: for he shall save his people from their sins. Matthew 1:21

1) Neatly trace the letters.
2) On the lines provided, copy the letters in your neatest handwriting.

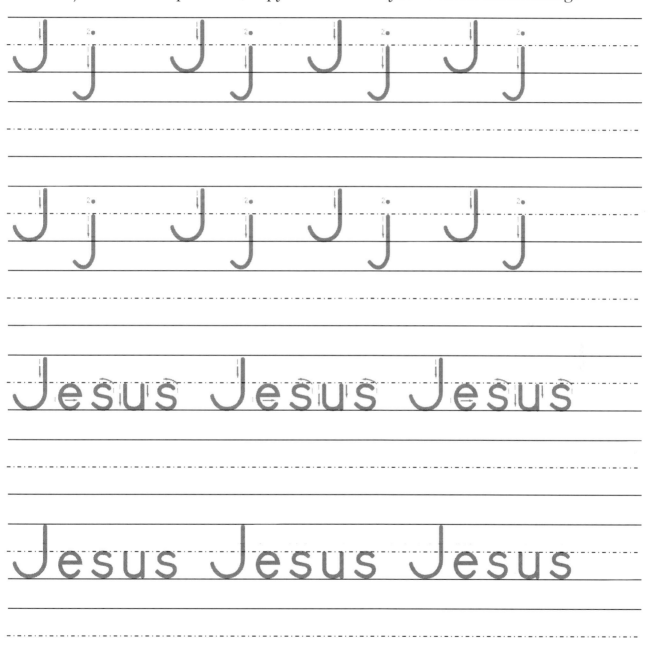

THE LETTER K

The **king** answered unto Daniel, and said, "Of a truth it is, that your God is a God of gods, and a Lord of kings, and a revealer of secrets, seeing that thou couldest reveal this secret." Daniel 2:47

1) Neatly trace the letters.
2) On the lines provided, copy the letters in your neatest handwriting.

Kk Kk Kk Kk

Kk Kk Kk Kk

King King King

King King King

THE LETTER L

The next day John seeth Jesus coming unto him, and saith, "Behold the **Lamb** of God, who taketh away the sin of the world."
John 1:29

1) Neatly trace the letters.
2) On the lines provided, copy the letters in your neatest handwriting.

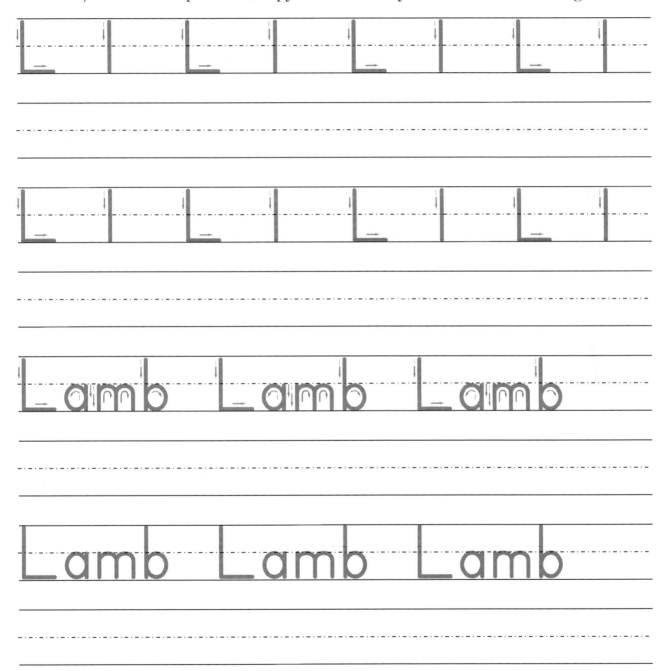

THE LETTER M

And they came with haste, and found **Mary**, and Joseph, and the babe lying in a manger. Luke 2:16

1) Neatly trace the letters.
2) On the lines provided, copy the letters in your neatest handwriting.

THE LETTER N

And God blessed **Noah** and his sons, and said unto them, "Be fruitful, and multiply, and replenish the earth." Genesis 9:1

1) Neatly trace the letters.
2) On the lines provided, copy the letters in your neatest handwriting.

THE LETTER O

Then Peter and the other apostles answered and said, "We ought to **obey** God rather than men." Acts 5:29

1) Neatly trace the letters.
2) On the lines provided, copy the letters in your neatest handwriting.

Oo Oo Oo Oo

Oo Oo Oo Oo

Obey Obey Obey

Obey Obey Obey

THE LETTER P

Rejoice evermore. **Pray** without ceasing. In everything give thanks, for this is the will of God in Christ Jesus concerning you.
1 Thessalonians 5:16-18

1) Neatly trace the letters.
2) On the lines provided, copy the letters in your neatest handwriting.

Pp Pp Pp Pp Pp

Pp Pp Pp Pp Pp

Pray Pray Pray

Pray Pray Pray

THE LETTER Q

The words of wise men are heard in **quiet** more than the cry of him that ruleth among fools. Ecclesiastes 9:17

1) Neatly trace the letters.
2) On the lines provided, copy the letters in your neatest handwriting.

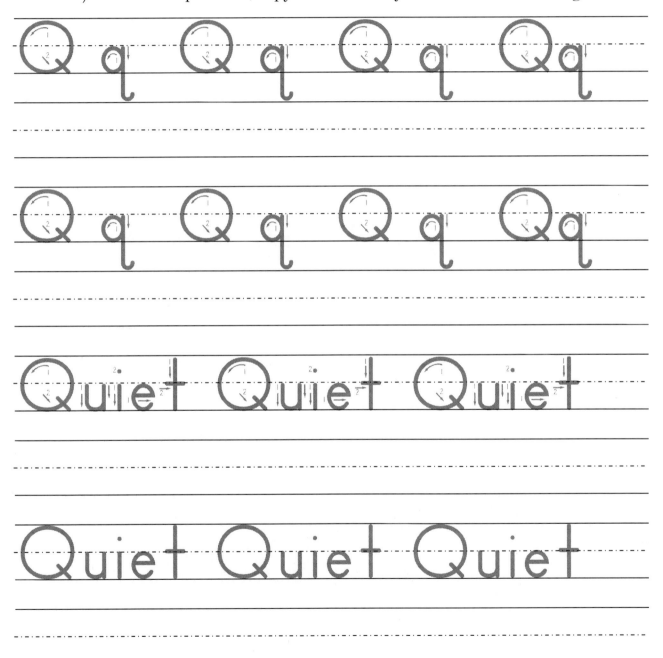

THE LETTER R

He is not here: for he is **risen**, as he said. Come; see the place where the Lord lay. Matthew 28:6

1) Neatly trace the letters.
2) On the lines provided, copy the letters in your neatest handwriting.

Rr Rr Rr Rr Rr

Rr Rr Rr Rr Rr

Risen Risen Risen

Risen Risen Risen

THE LETTER S

My **sheep** hear my voice, and I know them, and they follow me.
John 10:27

1) Neatly trace the letters.
2) On the lines provided, copy the letters in your neatest handwriting.

Ss Ss Ss Ss

Ss Ss Ss Ss

Sheep Sheep Sheep

Sheep Sheep Sheep

THE LETTER T

Jesus saith unto him, "I am the way, the **truth**, and the life: no man cometh unto the Father, but by me." John 14:6

1) Neatly trace the letters.
2) On the lines provided, copy the letters in your neatest handwriting.

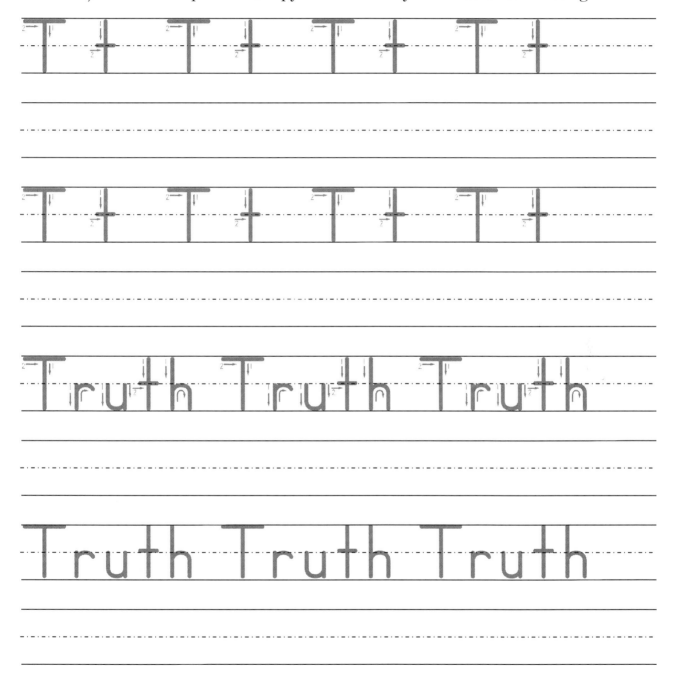

THE LETTER U

Unto thee, O my strength, will I sing: for God is my defense, and the God of my mercy. Psalm 59:17

1) Neatly trace the letters.
2) On the lines provided, copy the letters in your neatest handwriting.

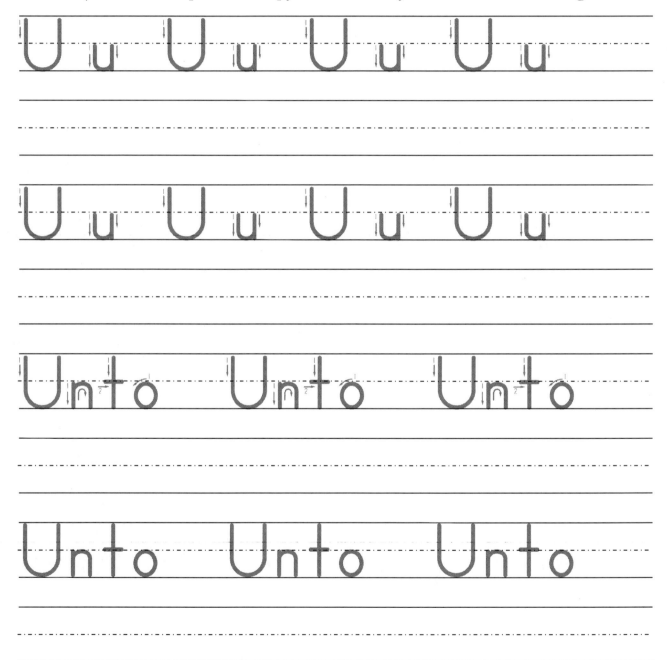

THE LETTER V

When Moses saw it, he wondered at the sight: and as he drew near to behold it, the **voice** of the Lord came unto him, Acts 7:31

1) Neatly trace the letters.
2) On the lines provided, copy the letters in your neatest handwriting.

Vv Vv Vv Vv Vv

Vv Vv Vv Vv Vv

Voice Voice Voice

Voice Voice Voice

THE LETTER W

But they that **wait** upon the LORD shall renew their strength; they shall mount up with wings as eagles; they shall run, and not be weary; and they shall walk, and not faint. Isaiah 40:31

1) Neatly trace the letters.
2) On the lines provided, copy the letters in your neatest handwriting.

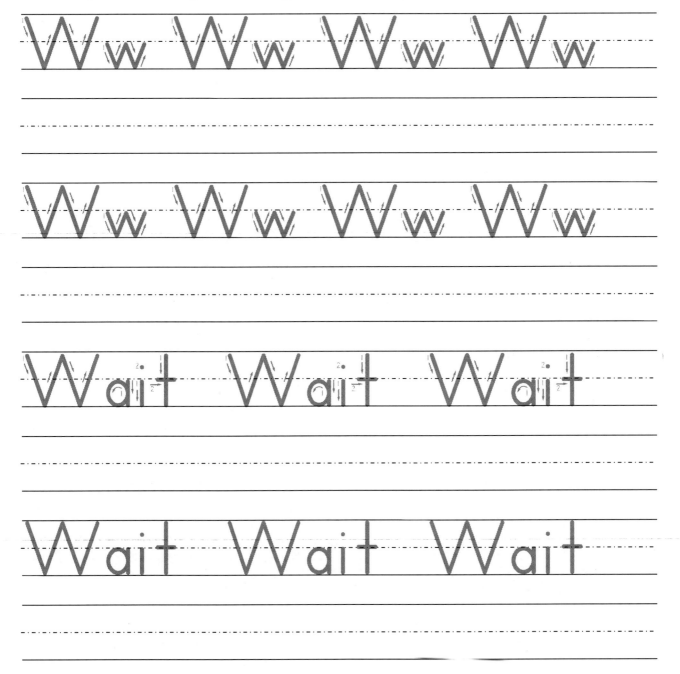

THE LETTER X

I also and my maidens will fast likewise; and so will I go in unto the king (King **Xerxes**), which is not according to the law: and if I perish, I perish. Esther 4:16

1) Neatly trace the letters.
2) On the lines provided, copy the letters in your neatest handwriting.

Xx Xx Xx Xx Xx

Xx Xx Xx Xx Xx

Xerxes Xerxes Xerxes

Xerxes Xerxes Xerxes

THE LETTER Y

Take My **yoke** upon you and learn of Me, for I am meek and lowly in heart, and ye shall find rest unto your souls. For My **yoke** is easy, and My burden is light. Matthew 11:28-30

1) Neatly trace the letters.
2) On the lines provided, copy the letters in your neatest handwriting.

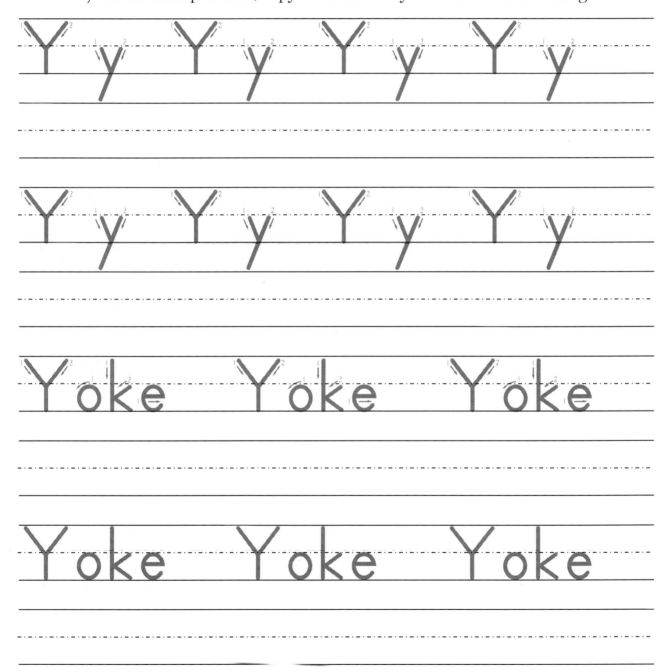

42

THE LETTER Z

Praise the Lord, O Jerusalem! Praise thy God, O Zion!
Psalm 147:12

1) Neatly trace the letters.
2) On the lines provided, copy the letters in your neatest handwriting.

Zz Zz Zz Zz Zz

Zz Zz Zz Zz Zz

Zion   Zion   Zion

Zion   Zion   Zion

REVIEWING

REVIEWING THE LETTERS

Copy the letters as neatly as you can.

Aa Bb Cc Dd Ee Ff Gg

Hh Ii Jj Kk Ll Mm Nn Oo

Pp Qq Rr Ss Tt Uu Vv

Ww Xx Yy Zz

REVIEWING THE LETTERS

Copy the letters as neatly as you can.

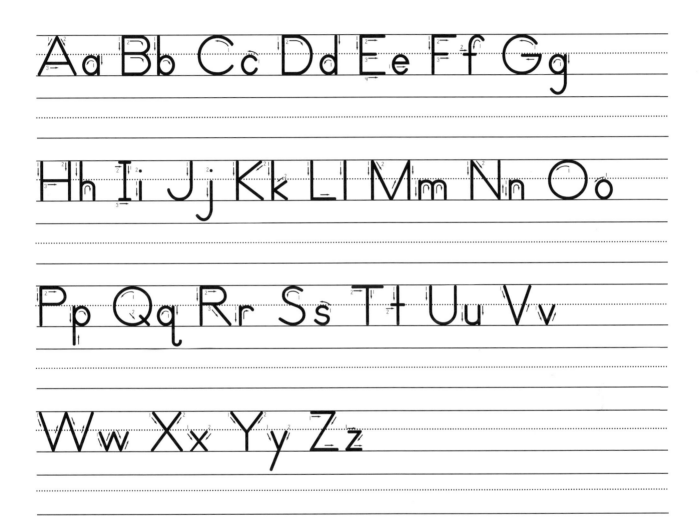

REVIEWING THE LETTERS

Copy the letters as neatly as you can.

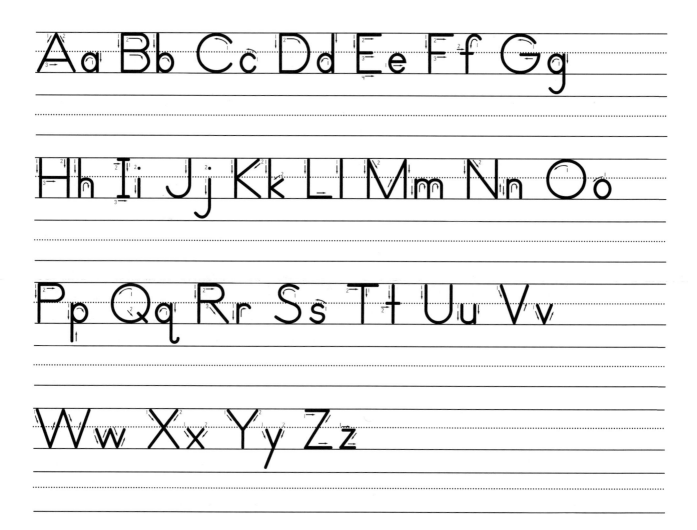

REVIEWING THE LETTERS

Copy the letters as neatly as you can.

Aa Bb Cc Dd Ee Ff Gg

Hh Ii Jj Kk Ll Mm Nn Oo

Pp Qq Rr Ss Tt Uu Vv

Ww Xx Yy Zz

WRITING NUMBERS

FORMING NUMBERS

Trace the numbers as neatly as you can.

Copy the numbers onto the lines provided.

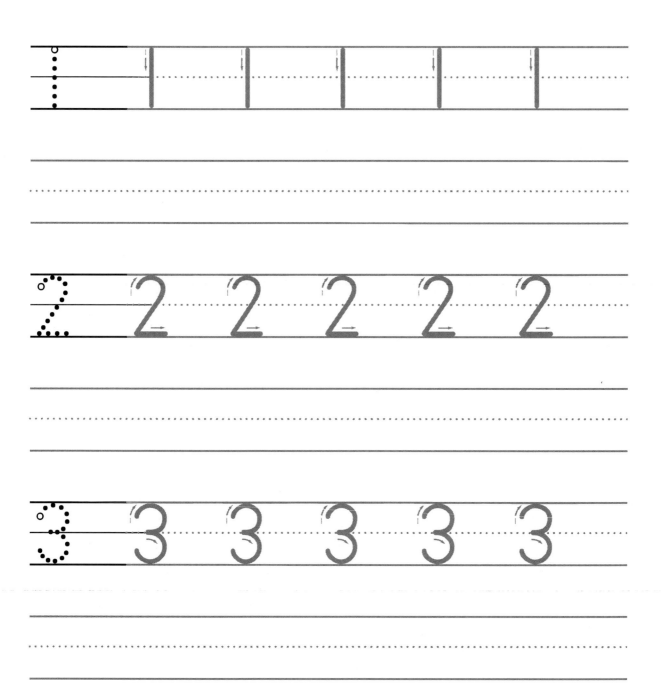

4 4 4 4 4

5 5 5 5 5

6 6 6 6 6

7 7 7 7 7

WRITING NUMBERS 0 AND 1

Copy the numbers as neatly as you can.

WRITING NUMBERS 2 AND 3

Copy the numbers as neatly as you can.

2 2 2 2 2 2 2 2

2 2 2 2 2 2 2 2

3 3 3 3 3 3 3 3

3 3 3 3 3 3 3 3

WRITING NUMBERS 4 AND 5

Copy the numbers as neatly as you can.

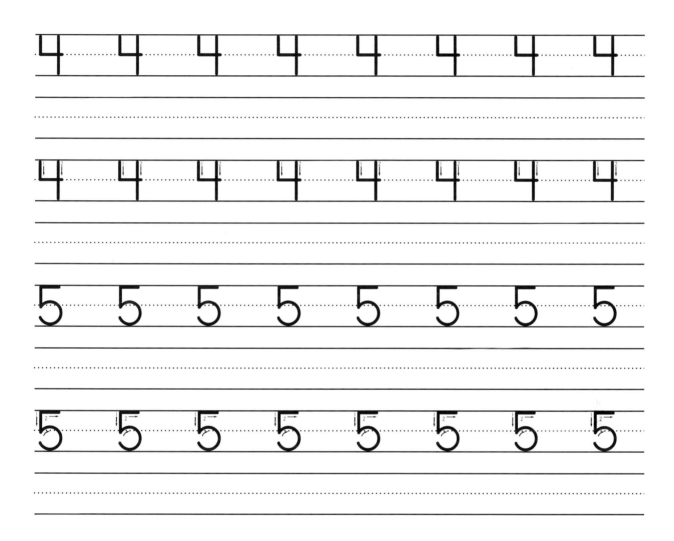

WRITING NUMBERS 6 AND 7

Copy the numbers as neatly as you can.

6 6 6 6 6 6 6 6

6 6 6 6 6 6 6 6

7 7 7 7 7 7 7 7

7 7 7 7 7 7 7 7

WRITING NUMBERS 8 AND 9

Copy the numbers as neatly as you can.

REVIEWING THE NUMBERS 0 TO 9

Copy the numbers as neatly as you can.

0 1 2 3 4 5 6 7 8 9

0 1 2 3 4 5 6 7 8 9

0 1 2 3 4 5 6 7 8 9

0 1 2 3 4 5 6 7 8 9

WRITING SCRIPTURE

DAY 1: GENESIS 1:1 WORD PRACTICE

Copy the words below.

beginning

created

heaven

earth

Genesis 1:1

DAY 2: GENESIS 1:1 WORD PRACTICE

Copy the words below.

beginning

created

heaven

earth

Genesis 1:1

DAY 3: GENESIS 1:1 WORD PRACTICE

Copy the words below.

beginning

created

heaven

earth

Genesis 1:1

DAY 4: GENESIS 1:1

Copy the Scripture onto the lines provided.
Remember to write as neatly as you can.

In the beginning God

created the heaven

and the earth.

Genesis 1:1

DAY 1: ISAIAH 9:6 WORD PRACTICE

Copy the words below.

child

born

son

given

Isaiah 9:6

DAY 2: ISAIAH 9:6 WORD PRACTICE

Copy the words below.

child

born

son

given

Isaiah 9:6

DAY 3: ISAIAH 9:6 WORD PRACTICE

Copy the words below.

child

born

son

given

Isaiah 9:6

DAY 4: ISAIAH 9:6

Copy the Scripture onto the lines provided.
Remember to write as neatly as you can.

For unto us a child is

born, unto us a son is

given.

Isaiah 9:6

DAY 1: JOHN 10:27 WORD PRACTICE

Copy the words below.

sheep

voice

know

follow

John 10:27

DAY 2: JOHN 10:27 WORD PRACTICE

Copy the words below.

sheep

voice

know

follow

John 10:27

DAY 3: JOHN 10:27 WORD PRACTICE

Copy the words below.

sheep

voice

know

follow

John 10:27

DAY 4: JOHN 10:27

Copy the Scripture onto the lines provided.
Remember to write as neatly as you can.

My sheep hear My voice

and I know them, and

they follow Me.

John 10:27

DAY 1: ISAIAH 6:3 WORD PRACTICE

Copy the words below.

holy

Lord

host

glory

Isaiah 6:3

DAY 2: ISAIAH 6:3 WORD PRACTICE

Copy the words below.

holy

Lord

host

glory

Isaiah 6:3

DAY 3: ISAIAH 6:3 WORD PRACTICE

Copy the words below.

holy

Lord

host

glory

Isaiah 6:3

DAY 4: ISAIAH 6:3

Copy the Scripture onto the lines provided.
Remember to write as neatly as you can.

Holy, holy, holy is the

Lord of hosts. The

earth is full of His glory.

Isaiah 6:3

Made in United States
Orlando, FL
07 September 2022

22120330R00050